☆☆☆☆☆

MOVIE REVIEW JOURNAL

For Kids

☆☆☆☆☆

This journal belongs to:

_____

_____

Phone:_____

Email:_____

Movie Review Journal For Kids

ISBN: 9781793254580

Printed in the USA

See the wide-ranging collection of
GOLDING NOTEBOOKS
now available on Amazon.

MOVIES TO WATCH

1. _____
2. _____
3. _____
4. _____
5. _____
6. _____
7. _____
8. _____
9. _____
10. _____
11. _____
12. _____
13. _____
14. _____
15. _____
16. _____
17. _____
18. _____
19. _____
20. _____

MOVIES TO WATCH

21. _____
22. _____
23. _____
24. _____
25. _____
26. _____
27. _____
28. _____
29. _____
30. _____
31. _____
32. _____
33. _____
34. _____
35. _____
36. _____
37. _____
38. _____
39. _____
40. _____

MOVIES TO WATCH

41. _____
42. _____
43. _____
44. _____
45. _____
46. _____
47. _____
48. _____
49. _____
50. _____
51. _____
52. _____
53. _____
54. _____
55. _____
56. _____
57. _____
58. _____
59. _____
60. _____

MOVIES TO WATCH

61. _____
62. _____
63. _____
64. _____
65. _____
66. _____
67. _____
68. _____
69. _____
70. _____
71. _____
72. _____
73. _____
74. _____
75. _____
76. _____
77. _____
78. _____
79. _____
80. _____

MOVIES TO WATCH

81. _____
82. _____
83. _____
84. _____
85. _____
86. _____
87. _____
88. _____
89. _____
90. _____
91. _____
92. _____
93. _____
94. _____
95. _____
96. _____
97. _____
98. _____
99. _____
100. _____

My TOP 10 Movies

List down your most favorite movies,
#1 being your most favorite of all.

#1

#2

#3

#4

#5

#6

#7

#8

#9

#10

My **TOP 10** Favorite
Actors & Actresses

List down your most favorite actors and actresses,
#1 being your most favorite of all.

#1

#2

#3

#4

#5

#6

#7

#8

#9

#10

Title:

Date: _____

Where I watched it:

_____

Who I watched with:

_____

_____

My Favorite Character:

_____

My Favorite Scene:

_____

_____

_____

_____

My Favorite Line:

"

"

My Favorite Song:

_____

MOVIE GENRE
What kind of movie was it?

- [ ] Animation/Cartoon
- [ ] Comedy
- [ ] Science Fiction
- [ ] Action/Adventure
- [ ] Fantasy/Superhero
- [ ] Horror/Suspense Thriller
- [ ] Drama
- [ ] Musical
- [ ] Romantic Comedy
- [ ] Documentary

popcorn

My thoughts:

_____

_____

_____

_____

_____

_____

_____

_____

_____

_____

MY RATING
How did you like the movie?

☆ ☆ ☆ ☆ ☆

Title:

Date: _____

Where I watched it:

_____

Who I watched with:

_____

_____

My Favorite Character:

_____

My Favorite Scene:

_____

_____

_____

My Favorite Line:

"

    "

My Favorite Song:

_____

MOVIE GENRE

What kind of movie was it?

- ☐ Animation/Cartoon
- ☐ Comedy
- ☐ Science Fiction
- ☐ Action/Adventure
- ☐ Fantasy/Superhero
- ☐ Horror/Suspense Thriller
- ☐ Drama
- ☐ Musical
- ☐ Romantic Comedy
- ☐ Documentary

My thoughts:

_____

_____

_____

_____

_____

_____

_____

_____

_____

MY RATING

How did you like the movie?

☆ ☆ ☆ ☆ ☆

Title:

Date: _____

Where I watched it:

_____

Who I watched with:

_____

_____

My Favorite Character:

_____

My Favorite Scene:

_____

_____

_____

My Favorite Line:

"

                          "

My Favorite Song:

_____

MOVIE GENRE
What kind of movie was it?

- [ ] Animation/Cartoon
- [ ] Comedy
- [ ] Science Fiction
- [ ] Action/Adventure
- [ ] Fantasy/Superhero
- [ ] Horror/Suspense Thriller
- [ ] Drama
- [ ] Musical
- [ ] Romantic Comedy
- [ ] Documentary

popcorn

My thoughts:

_____

_____

_____

_____

_____

_____

_____

_____

_____

_____

_____

MY RATING
How did you like the movie?

☆ ☆ ☆ ☆ ☆

Title:

Date: _____

Where I watched it:
_____

Who I watched with:
_____
_____

My Favorite Character:
_____

My Favorite Scene:
_____
_____
_____
_____

My Favorite Line:

"
                              "

My Favorite Song:
_____

MOVIE GENRE
What kind of movie was it?

- [ ] Animation/Cartoon
- [ ] Comedy
- [ ] Science Fiction
- [ ] Action/Adventure
- [ ] Fantasy/Superhero
- [ ] Horror/Suspense Thriller
- [ ] Drama
- [ ] Musical
- [ ] Romantic Comedy
- [ ] Documentary

popcorn

My thoughts:
_____
_____
_____
_____
_____
_____
_____
_____

MY RATING
How did you like the movie?

☆ ☆ ☆ ☆ ☆

Title:

Date: _____

Where I watched it:

_____

Who I watched with:

_____

_____

My Favorite Character:

_____

My Favorite Scene:

_____

_____

_____

_____

My Favorite Line:

"

   "

My Favorite Song:

_____

MOVIE GENRE
What kind of movie was it?

- ☐ Animation/Cartoon
- ☐ Comedy
- ☐ Science Fiction
- ☐ Action/Adventure
- ☐ Fantasy/Superhero
- ☐ Horror/Suspense Thriller
- ☐ Drama
- ☐ Musical
- ☐ Romantic Comedy
- ☐ Documentary

My thoughts:

_____

_____

_____

_____

_____

_____

_____

_____

_____

_____

MY RATING
How did you like the movie?

☆ ☆ ☆ ☆ ☆

Title:

Date: _____

Where I watched it:

_____

Who I watched with:

_____

_____

My Favorite Character:

_____

My Favorite Scene:

_____

_____

_____

_____

My Favorite Line:

"

»

My Favorite Song:

_____

MOVIE GENRE
What kind of movie was it?

☐ Animation/Cartoon
☐ Comedy
☐ Science Fiction
☐ Action/Adventure
☐ Fantasy/Superhero
☐ Horror/Suspense Thriller
☐ Drama
☐ Musical
☐ Romantic Comedy
☐ Documentary

My thoughts:

_____

_____

_____

_____

_____

_____

_____

_____

_____

_____

MY RATING
How did you like the movie?

☆ ☆ ☆ ☆ ☆

Title:

Date: _____

Where I watched it:

_____

Who I watched with:

_____

_____

My Favorite Character:

_____

My Favorite Scene:

_____

_____

_____

My Favorite Line:

> "
>
>   "

My Favorite Song:

_____

MOVIE GENRE
What kind of movie was it?

- [ ] Animation/Cartoon
- [ ] Comedy
- [ ] Science Fiction
- [ ] Action/Adventure
- [ ] Fantasy/Superhero
- [ ] Horror/Suspense Thriller
- [ ] Drama
- [ ] Musical
- [ ] Romantic Comedy
- [ ] Documentary

My thoughts:

_____

_____

_____

_____

_____

_____

_____

_____

MY RATING
How did you like the movie?

☆ ☆ ☆ ☆ ☆

Title:

Date: _____

Where I watched it:
_____

Who I watched with:
_____
_____

My Favorite Character:
_____

My Favorite Scene:
_____
_____
_____
_____

My Favorite Line:

"
"

My Favorite Song:
_____

MOVIE GENRE
What kind of movie was it?

- ☐ Animation/Cartoon
- ☐ Comedy
- ☐ Science Fiction
- ☐ Action/Adventure
- ☐ Fantasy/Superhero
- ☐ Horror/Suspense Thriller
- ☐ Drama
- ☐ Musical
- ☐ Romantic Comedy
- ☐ Documentary

My thoughts:
_____
_____
_____
_____
_____
_____
_____
_____

MY RATING
How did you like the movie?

☆ ☆ ☆ ☆ ☆

Title:

Date: _____

Where I watched it:

_____

Who I watched with:

_____

_____

My Favorite Character:

_____

My Favorite Scene:

_____

_____

_____

_____

My Favorite Line:

"

"

My Favorite Song:

_____

MOVIE GENRE

What kind of movie was it?

- [ ] Animation/Cartoon
- [ ] Comedy
- [ ] Science Fiction
- [ ] Action/Adventure
- [ ] Fantasy/Superhero
- [ ] Horror/Suspense Thriller
- [ ] Drama
- [ ] Musical
- [ ] Romantic Comedy
- [ ] Documentary

popcorn

My thoughts:

_____

_____

_____

_____

_____

_____

_____

_____

_____

MY RATING

How did you like the movie?

☆ ☆ ☆ ☆ ☆

Title:

Date: _____

Where I watched it:
_____

Who I watched with:
_____
_____

My Favorite Character:
_____

My Favorite Scene:
_____
_____
_____
_____
_____

My Favorite Line:
"

                    ''

My Favorite Song:
_____

MOVIE GENRE
What kind of movie was it?

- ☐ Animation/Cartoon
- ☐ Comedy
- ☐ Science Fiction
- ☐ Action/Adventure
- ☐ Fantasy/Superhero
- ☐ Horror/Suspense Thriller
- ☐ Drama
- ☐ Musical
- ☐ Romantic Comedy
- ☐ Documentary

My thoughts:
_____
_____
_____
_____
_____
_____
_____
_____
_____

MY RATING
How did you like the movie?

☆ ☆ ☆ ☆ ☆

Title:

Date: _____

Where I watched it:

_____

Who I watched with:

_____

_____

My Favorite Character:

_____

My Favorite Scene:

_____

_____

_____

My Favorite Line:

"

"

My Favorite Song:

_____

MOVIE GENRE

What kind of movie was it?

- [ ] Animation/Cartoon
- [ ] Comedy
- [ ] Science Fiction
- [ ] Action/Adventure
- [ ] Fantasy/Superhero
- [ ] Horror/Suspense Thriller
- [ ] Drama
- [ ] Musical
- [ ] Romantic Comedy
- [ ] Documentary

My thoughts:

_____

_____

_____

_____

_____

_____

_____

_____

_____

MY RATING

How did you like the movie?

☆ ☆ ☆ ☆ ☆

Title:

Date: _____

Where I watched it:
_____
_____

Who I watched with:
_____
_____
_____

My Favorite Character:
_____

My Favorite Scene:
_____
_____
_____
_____
_____

My Favorite Line:

"

"

My Favorite Song:
_____

MOVIE GENRE
What kind of movie was it?

- ☐ Animation/Cartoon
- ☐ Comedy
- ☐ Science Fiction
- ☐ Action/Adventure
- ☐ Fantasy/Superhero
- ☐ Horror/Suspense Thriller
- ☐ Drama
- ☐ Musical
- ☐ Romantic Comedy
- ☐ Documentary

My thoughts:
_____
_____
_____
_____
_____
_____
_____
_____
_____

MY RATING
How did you like the movie?

☆ ☆ ☆ ☆ ☆

Title:

Date: _____

Where I watched it:

_____

Who I watched with:

_____

_____

My Favorite Character:

_____

My Favorite Scene:

_____

_____

_____

My Favorite Line:

"

"

My Favorite Song:

_____

What kind of movie was it?
- [ ] Animation/Cartoon
- [ ] Comedy
- [ ] Science Fiction
- [ ] Action/Adventure
- [ ] Fantasy/Superhero
- [ ] Horror/Suspense Thriller
- [ ] Drama
- [ ] Musical
- [ ] Romantic Comedy
- [ ] Documentary

popcorn

My thoughts:

_____

_____

_____

_____

_____

_____

_____

_____

_____

MY RATING

How did you like the movie?

☆ ☆ ☆ ☆ ☆

Title:

Date: _____

Where I watched it:
_____
_____

Who I watched with:
_____
_____

My Favorite Character:
_____

My Favorite Scene:
_____
_____
_____
_____

My Favorite Line:

"

"

My Favorite Song:
_____

MOVIE GENRE
What kind of movie was it?

- ☐ Animation/Cartoon
- ☐ Comedy
- ☐ Science Fiction
- ☐ Action/Adventure
- ☐ Fantasy/Superhero
- ☐ Horror/Suspense Thriller
- ☐ Drama
- ☐ Musical
- ☐ Romantic Comedy
- ☐ Documentary

My thoughts:
_____
_____
_____
_____
_____
_____
_____
_____

MY RATING
How did you like the movie?

☆ ☆ ☆ ☆ ☆

Title:

Date: _____

Where I watched it:

_____

Who I watched with:

_____

_____

My Favorite Character:

_____

My Favorite Scene:

_____

_____

_____

My Favorite Line:

"

"

My Favorite Song:

_____

What kind of movie was it?

☐ Animation/Cartoon
☐ Comedy
☐ Science Fiction
☐ Action/Adventure
☐ Fantasy/Superhero
☐ Horror/Suspense Thriller
☐ Drama
☐ Musical
☐ Romantic Comedy
☐ Documentary

popcorn

My thoughts:

_____

_____

_____

_____

_____

_____

_____

_____

_____

MY RATING

How did you like the movie?

☆ ☆ ☆ ☆ ☆

Title:

Date: _____

Where I watched it:

_____

Who I watched with:

_____

_____

My Favorite Character:

_____

My Favorite Scene:

_____

_____

_____

My Favorite Line:

"
_____
_____
_____
                    "

My Favorite Song:

_____

MOVIE GENRE
What kind of movie was it?

☐ Animation/Cartoon
☐ Comedy
☐ Science Fiction
☐ Action/Adventure
☐ Fantasy/Superhero
☐ Horror/Suspense Thriller
☐ Drama
☐ Musical
☐ Romantic Comedy
☐ Documentary

popcorn

My thoughts:

_____
_____
_____
_____
_____
_____
_____
_____

MY RATING
How did you like the movie?

☆ ☆ ☆ ☆ ☆

Title:

Date: _____

Where I watched it:

_____

Who I watched with:

_____

_____

My Favorite Character:

_____

My Favorite Scene:

_____

_____

_____

_____

My Favorite Line:

"

"

My Favorite Song:

_____

MOVIE GENRE
What kind of movie was it?

- [ ] Animation/Cartoon
- [ ] Comedy
- [ ] Science Fiction
- [ ] Action/Adventure
- [ ] Fantasy/Superhero
- [ ] Horror/Suspense Thriller
- [ ] Drama
- [ ] Musical
- [ ] Romantic Comedy
- [ ] Documentary

popcorn

My thoughts:

_____

_____

_____

_____

_____

_____

_____

_____

_____

_____

MY RATING
How did you like the movie?

☆ ☆ ☆ ☆ ☆

Title: _____

Date: _____

Where I watched it:

_____

Who I watched with:

_____
_____

My Favorite Character:

_____

My Favorite Scene:

_____
_____
_____
_____

My Favorite Line:

"

                                    "

My Favorite Song:

_____

MOVIE GENRE
What kind of movie was it?

- ☐ Animation/Cartoon
- ☐ Comedy
- ☐ Science Fiction
- ☐ Action/Adventure
- ☐ Fantasy/Superhero
- ☐ Horror/Suspense Thriller
- ☐ Drama
- ☐ Musical
- ☐ Romantic Comedy
- ☐ Documentary

popcorn

My thoughts:

_____
_____
_____
_____
_____
_____
_____
_____
_____
_____

MY RATING
How did you like the movie?

☆ ☆ ☆ ☆ ☆

Title:

Date:

When **I** watched it:

_____

Who **I** watched with:

_____
_____
_____

My Favorite Character:

_____

My Favorite Scene:

_____
_____
_____
_____

My Favorite Line:

" "
>>

My Favorite Song:

_____

MOVIE GENRE
What kind of movie was it?

- [ ] Animation/Cartoon
- [ ] Comedy
- [ ] Science Fiction
- [ ] Action/Adventure
- [ ] Fantasy/Superhero
- [ ] Horror/Suspense Thriller
- [ ] Drama
- [ ] Musical
- [ ] Romantic Comedy
- [ ] Documentary

My thoughts:

popcorn

_____
_____
_____
_____
_____
_____
_____
_____
_____
_____

MY RATING
How did you like the movie?

☆ ☆ ☆ ☆ ☆

Title:

Date: _____

Where I watched it: _____

_____

Who I watched with: _____

_____

_____

My Favorite Character:

_____

My Favorite Scene:

_____

_____

_____

_____

My Favorite Line:

"

"

My Favorite Song:

_____

MOVIE GENRE
What kind of movie was it?

☐ Animation/Cartoon
☐ Comedy
☐ Science Fiction
☐ Action/Adventure
☐ Fantasy/Superhero
☐ Horror/Suspense Thriller
☐ Drama
☐ Musical
☐ Romantic Comedy
☐ Documentary

My thoughts:

_____

_____

_____

_____

_____

_____

_____

_____

_____

_____

_____

MY RATING
How did you like the movie?

☆ ☆ ☆ ☆ ☆

Title:

Date:

Where I watched it:

_____

Who I watched with:

_____

_____

My Favorite Character:

_____

My Favorite Scene:

_____

_____

_____

My Favorite Line:

> "

> "

My Favorite Song:

_____

MOVIE GENRE
What kind of movie was it?

- [ ] Animation/Cartoon
- [ ] Comedy
- [ ] Science Fiction
- [ ] Action/Adventure
- [ ] Fantasy/Superhero
- [ ] Horror/Suspense Thriller
- [ ] Drama
- [ ] Musical
- [ ] Romantic Comedy
- [ ] Documentary

My thoughts:

_____

_____

_____

_____

_____

_____

_____

_____

MY RATING
How did you like the movie?

☆ ☆ ☆ ☆ ☆

Title:

Date: _____

Where I watched it:

_____

Who I watched with:

_____

_____

My Favorite Character:

_____

My Favorite Scene:

_____

_____

_____

_____

My Favorite Line:

"

                          "

My Favorite Song:

_____

MOVIE GENRE
What kind of movie was it?

- ☐ Animation/Cartoon
- ☐ Comedy
- ☐ Science Fiction
- ☐ Action/Adventure
- ☐ Fantasy/Superhero
- ☐ Horror/Suspense Thriller
- ☐ Drama
- ☐ Musical
- ☐ Romantic Comedy
- ☐ Documentary

My thoughts:

_____

_____

_____

_____

_____

_____

_____

_____

_____

MY RATING
How did you like the movie?

☆ ☆ ☆ ☆ ☆

Title:

Date:

Where I watched it:

Who I watched with:

My Favorite Character:

My Favorite Scene:

My Favorite Line:

"

"

My Favorite Song:

MOVIE GENRE
What kind of movie was it?

- [ ] Animation/Cartoon
- [ ] Comedy
- [ ] Science Fiction
- [ ] Action/Adventure
- [ ] Fantasy/Superhero
- [ ] Horror/Suspense Thriller
- [ ] Drama
- [ ] Musical
- [ ] Romantic Comedy
- [ ] Documentary

popcorn

My thoughts:

MY RATING
How did you like the movie?

☆ ☆ ☆ ☆ ☆

Title:

Date: _____

Where I watched it:

_____

Who I watched with:

_____

_____

My Favorite Character:

_____

My Favorite Scene:

_____

_____

_____

_____

My Favorite Line:

"

                              "

My Favorite Song:

_____

MOVIE GENRE

What kind of movie was it?

- ☐ Animation/Cartoon
- ☐ Comedy
- ☐ Science Fiction
- ☐ Action/Adventure
- ☐ Fantasy/Superhero
- ☐ Horror/Suspense Thriller
- ☐ Drama
- ☐ Musical
- ☐ Romantic Comedy
- ☐ Documentary

My thoughts:

_____

_____

_____

_____

_____

_____

_____

_____

_____

MY RATING

How did you like the movie?

☆ ☆ ☆ ☆ ☆

Title:

Date:

Where I watched it:

_____

Who I watched with:

_____

_____

My Favorite Character:

_____

My Favorite Scene:

_____

_____

_____

_____

My Favorite Line:

> "
>
> "

My Favorite Song:

_____

MOVIE GENRE

What kind of movie was it?

- [ ] Animation/Cartoon
- [ ] Comedy
- [ ] Science Fiction
- [ ] Action/Adventure
- [ ] Fantasy/Superhero
- [ ] Horror/Suspense Thriller
- [ ] Drama
- [ ] Musical
- [ ] Romantic Comedy
- [ ] Documentary

popcorn

My thoughts:

_____

_____

_____

_____

_____

_____

_____

_____

_____

_____

_____

MY RATING

How did you like the movie?

☆ ☆ ☆ ☆ ☆

Title:

Date: _____

Where I watched it:

_____

Who I watched with:

_____

_____

My Favorite Character:

_____

My Favorite Scene:

_____

_____

_____

_____

My Favorite Line:

"

           "

My Favorite Song:

_____

MOVIE GENRE

What kind of movie was it?

- ☐ Animation/Cartoon
- ☐ Comedy
- ☐ Science Fiction
- ☐ Action/Adventure
- ☐ Fantasy/Superhero
- ☐ Horror/Suspense Thriller
- ☐ Drama
- ☐ Musical
- ☐ Romantic Comedy
- ☐ Documentary

popcorn

My thoughts:

_____

_____

_____

_____

_____

_____

_____

_____

_____

MY RATING

How did you like the movie?

☆ ☆ ☆ ☆ ☆

Title:

Date:

Where I watched it:

_____

Who I watched with:

_____

_____

My Favorite Character:

_____

My Favorite Scene:

_____

_____

_____

_____

My Favorite Line:

> "

> "

My Favorite Song:

MOVIE GENRE
What kind of movie was it?

- [ ] Animation/Cartoon
- [ ] Comedy
- [ ] Science Fiction
- [ ] Action/Adventure
- [ ] Fantasy/Superhero
- [ ] Horror/Suspense Thriller
- [ ] Drama
- [ ] Musical
- [ ] Romantic Comedy
- [ ] Documentary

popcorn

My thoughts:

_____

_____

_____

_____

_____

_____

_____

_____

_____

MY RATING
How did you like the movie?

☆ ☆ ☆ ☆ ☆

Title:

Date: _____

Where I watched it:

_____

Who I watched with:

_____

_____

My Favorite Character:

_____

My Favorite Scene:

_____

_____

_____

_____

My Favorite Line:

"

"

My Favorite Song:

_____

MOVIE GENRE

What kind of movie was it?

- [ ] Animation/Cartoon
- [ ] Comedy
- [ ] Science Fiction
- [ ] Action/Adventure
- [ ] Fantasy/Superhero
- [ ] Horror/Suspense Thriller
- [ ] Drama
- [ ] Musical
- [ ] Romantic Comedy
- [ ] Documentary

My thoughts:

_____

_____

_____

_____

_____

_____

_____

_____

MY RATING

How did you like the movie?

☆ ☆ ☆ ☆ ☆

Title:

Date:

Where I watched it:

_____

Who I watched with:

_____

_____

My Favorite Character:

_____

My Favorite Scene:

_____

_____

_____

My Favorite Line:

"

                          "

My Favorite Song:

_____

MOVIE GENRE

What kind of movie was it?

☐ Animation/Cartoon
☐ Comedy
☐ Science Fiction
☐ Action/Adventure
☐ Fantasy/Superhero
☐ Horror/Suspense Thriller
☐ Drama
☐ Musical
☐ Romantic Comedy
☐ Documentary

popcorn

My thoughts:

_____

_____

_____

_____

_____

_____

_____

_____

MY RATING

How did you like the movie?

☆ ☆ ☆ ☆ ☆

Title: _____

Date: _____

Where I watched it: _____

_____

Who I watched with: _____

_____

_____

My Favorite Character: _____

_____

My Favorite Scene: _____

_____

_____

_____

My Favorite Line:

"
>>

My Favorite Song: _____

_____

MOVIE GENRE

What kind of movie was it?

- ☐ Animation/Cartoon
- ☐ Comedy
- ☐ Science Fiction
- ☐ Action/Adventure
- ☐ Fantasy/Superhero
- ☐ Horror/Suspense Thriller
- ☐ Drama
- ☐ Musical
- ☐ Romantic Comedy
- ☐ Documentary

My thoughts:

_____

_____

_____

_____

_____

_____

_____

_____

MY RATING

How did you like the movie?

☆ ☆ ☆ ☆ ☆

Title:

Date:

Where I watched it:

_____

Who I watched with:

_____

_____

My Favorite Character:

_____

My Favorite Scene:

_____

_____

_____

_____

My Favorite Line:

"

                                    "

My Favorite Song:

_____

MOVIE GENRE

What kind of movie was it?

- ☐ Animation/Cartoon
- ☐ Comedy
- ☐ Science Fiction
- ☐ Action/Adventure
- ☐ Fantasy/Superhero
- ☐ Horror/Suspense Thriller
- ☐ Drama
- ☐ Musical
- ☐ Romantic Comedy
- ☐ Documentary

My thoughts:

_____

_____

_____

_____

_____

_____

_____

_____

_____

MY RATING

How did you like the movie?

☆ ☆ ☆ ☆ ☆

Title:

Date: _____

Where I watched it:

_____

Who I watched with:

_____

_____

My Favorite Character:

_____

My Favorite Scene:

_____

_____

_____

_____

My Favorite Line:

"

"

My Favorite Song:

_____

MOVIE GENRE

What kind of movie was it?

- ☐ Animation/Cartoon
- ☐ Comedy
- ☐ Science Fiction
- ☐ Action/Adventure
- ☐ Fantasy/Superhero
- ☐ Horror/Suspense Thriller
- ☐ Drama
- ☐ Musical
- ☐ Romantic Comedy
- ☐ Documentary

popcorn

My thoughts:

_____

_____

_____

_____

_____

_____

_____

_____

MY RATING

How did you like the movie?

☆ ☆ ☆ ☆ ☆

Title:

Date:

Where I watched it:

_____

Who I watched with:

_____

_____

My Favorite Character:

_____

My Favorite Scene:

_____

_____

_____

My Favorite Line:

"

                              ''

My Favorite Song:

_____

MOVIE GENRE

What kind of movie was it?

- [ ] Animation/Cartoon
- [ ] Comedy
- [ ] Science Fiction
- [ ] Action/Adventure
- [ ] Fantasy/Superhero
- [ ] Horror/Suspense Thriller
- [ ] Drama
- [ ] Musical
- [ ] Romantic Comedy
- [ ] Documentary

popcorn

My thoughts:

_____

_____

_____

_____

_____

_____

_____

_____

_____

MY RATING

How did you like the movie?

☆ ☆ ☆ ☆ ☆

Title:

Date: _____

Where I watched it:
_____

Who I watched with:
_____
_____

My Favorite Character:
_____

My Favorite Scene:
_____
_____
_____

My Favorite Line:
> "
>
>   "

My Favorite Song:
_____

MOVIE GENRE
What kind of movie was it?

- [ ] Animation/Cartoon
- [ ] Comedy
- [ ] Science Fiction
- [ ] Action/Adventure
- [ ] Fantasy/Superhero
- [ ] Horror/Suspense Thriller
- [ ] Drama
- [ ] Musical
- [ ] Romantic Comedy
- [ ] Documentary

popcorn

My thoughts:
_____
_____
_____
_____
_____
_____
_____
_____
_____

MY RATING
How did you like the movie?

☆ ☆ ☆ ☆ ☆

Title: _____

Date: _____

Where I watched it:

_____

Who I watched with:

_____

_____

My Favorite Character:

_____

My Favorite Scene:

_____

_____

_____

_____

My Favorite Line:

"
                              "

My Favorite Song:

_____

MOVIE GENRE

What kind of movie was it?

- ☐ Animation/Cartoon
- ☐ Comedy
- ☐ Science Fiction
- ☐ Action/Adventure
- ☐ Fantasy/Superhero
- ☐ Horror/Suspense Thriller
- ☐ Drama
- ☐ Musical
- ☐ Romantic Comedy
- ☐ Documentary

popcorn

My thoughts:

_____
_____
_____
_____
_____
_____
_____
_____
_____
_____
_____
_____

MY RATING

How did you like the movie?

☆ ☆ ☆ ☆ ☆

Title:

Date: _____

Where I watched it:

_____

Who I watched with:

_____

_____

My Favorite Character:

_____

My Favorite Scene:

_____

_____

_____

_____

My Favorite Line:

"

                                    "

My Favorite Song:

MOVIE GENRE
What kind of movie was it?

- ☐ Animation/Cartoon
- ☐ Comedy
- ☐ Science Fiction
- ☐ Action/Adventure
- ☐ Fantasy/Superhero
- ☐ Horror/Suspense Thriller
- ☐ Drama
- ☐ Musical
- ☐ Romantic Comedy
- ☐ Documentary

popcorn

My thoughts:

_____

_____

_____

_____

_____

_____

_____

_____

_____

_____

MY RATING
How did you like the movie?

☆ ☆ ☆ ☆ ☆

Title:

Date: _____

Where I watched it:

_____

Who I watched with:

_____

_____

My Favorite Character:

_____

My Favorite Scene:

_____

_____

_____

_____

My Favorite Line:

"

                                    "

My Favorite Song:

_____

MOVIE GENRE

What kind of movie was it?

- ☐ Animation/Cartoon
- ☐ Comedy
- ☐ Science Fiction
- ☐ Action/Adventure
- ☐ Fantasy/Superhero
- ☐ Horror/Suspense Thriller
- ☐ Drama
- ☐ Musical
- ☐ Romantic Comedy
- ☐ Documentary

My thoughts:

_____

_____

_____

_____

_____

_____

_____

_____

MY RATING

How did you like the movie?

☆ ☆ ☆ ☆ ☆

MOVIE REVIEW JOURNAL FOR KIDS

Title:

Date: _____

Where I watched it: _____

Who I watched with: _____
_____
_____

My Favorite Character: _____
_____

My Favorite Scene: _____
_____
_____
_____
_____

My Favorite Line:

"
_____

"

My Favorite Song: _____
_____

MOVIE GENRE

What kind of movie was it?

- [ ] Animation/Cartoon
- [ ] Comedy
- [ ] Science Fiction
- [ ] Action/Adventure
- [ ] Fantasy/Superhero
- [ ] Horror/Suspense Thriller
- [ ] Drama
- [ ] Musical
- [ ] Romantic Comedy
- [ ] Documentary

popcorn

My thoughts:
_____
_____
_____
_____
_____
_____
_____
_____
_____
_____
_____

MY RATING

How did you like the movie?

☆ ☆ ☆ ☆ ☆

Title: _____

Date: _____

What kind of movie was it?

☐ Animation/Cartoon
☐ Comedy
☐ Science Fiction
☐ Action/Adventure
☐ Fantasy/Superhero
☐ Horror/Suspense Thriller
☐ Drama
☐ Musical
☐ Romantic Comedy
☐ Documentary

Where I watched it: _____

Who I watched with:

_____
_____
_____

My Favorite Character:

_____

My Favorite Scene:

_____
_____
_____
_____

My thoughts:

_____
_____
_____
_____
_____
_____
_____
_____
_____

popcorn

My Favorite Line:

"

"

My Favorite Song:

_____

MY RATING

How did you like the movie?

☆ ☆ ☆ ☆ ☆

Title:

Date: _____

Where I watched it:
_____

Who I watched with:
_____
_____

My Favorite Character:
_____

My Favorite Scene:
_____
_____
_____
_____

My Favorite Line:

"

"

My Favorite Song:
_____

MOVIE GENRE
What kind of movie was it?

☐ Animation/Cartoon
☐ Comedy
☐ Science Fiction
☐ Action/Adventure
☐ Fantasy/Superhero
☐ Horror/Suspense Thriller
☐ Drama
☐ Musical
☐ Romantic Comedy
☐ Documentary

My thoughts:
_____
_____
_____
_____
_____
_____
_____
_____
_____

MY RATING
How did you like the movie?

☆ ☆ ☆ ☆ ☆

Title:

Date: _____

Where I watched it:

_____

Who I watched with:

_____

_____

My Favorite Character:

_____

My Favorite Scene:

_____

_____

_____

My Favorite Line:

"

                          "

My Favorite Song:

_____

MOVIE GENRE

What kind of movie was it?

- [ ] Animation/Cartoon
- [ ] Comedy
- [ ] Science Fiction
- [ ] Action/Adventure
- [ ] Fantasy/Superhero
- [ ] Horror/Suspense Thriller
- [ ] Drama
- [ ] Musical
- [ ] Romantic Comedy
- [ ] Documentary

popcorn

My thoughts:

_____

_____

_____

_____

_____

_____

_____

_____

MY RATING

How did you like the movie?

☆ ☆ ☆ ☆ ☆

Title:

Date: _____

Where I watched it:

_____

Who I watched with:

_____

_____

My Favorite Character:

_____

My Favorite Scene:

_____

_____

_____

My Favorite Line:

"

"

My Favorite Song:

_____

MOVIE GENRE

What kind of movie was it?

☐ Animation/Cartoon
☐ Comedy
☐ Science Fiction
☐ Action/Adventure
☐ Fantasy/Superhero
☐ Horror/Suspense Thriller
☐ Drama
☐ Musical
☐ Romantic Comedy
☐ Documentary

popcorn

My thoughts:

_____
_____
_____
_____
_____
_____
_____
_____
_____
_____

MY RATING

How did you like the movie?

☆ ☆ ☆ ☆ ☆

Title:

Date:

Where I watched it:

_____

Who I watched with:

_____
_____

My Favorite Character:

_____

My Favorite Scene:

_____
_____
_____

My Favorite Line:

"

"

My Favorite Song:

_____

MOVIE GENRE

What kind of movie was it?

- [ ] Animation/Cartoon
- [ ] Comedy
- [ ] Science Fiction
- [ ] Action/Adventure
- [ ] Fantasy/Superhero
- [ ] Horror/Suspense Thriller
- [ ] Drama
- [ ] Musical
- [ ] Romantic Comedy
- [ ] Documentary

popcorn

My thoughts:

_____
_____
_____
_____
_____
_____
_____
_____
_____
_____
_____

MY RATING

How did you like the movie?

☆ ☆ ☆ ☆ ☆

Title:

Date: _____

Where I watched it:

_____

Who I watched with:

_____

_____

My Favorite Character:

_____

My Favorite Scene:

_____

_____

_____

_____

My Favorite Line:

"

                                    "

My Favorite Song:

_____

MOVIE GENRE
What kind of movie was it?

- ☐ Animation/Cartoon
- ☐ Comedy
- ☐ Science Fiction
- ☐ Action/Adventure
- ☐ Fantasy/Superhero
- ☐ Horror/Suspense Thriller
- ☐ Drama
- ☐ Musical
- ☐ Romantic Comedy
- ☐ Documentary

My thoughts:

_____

_____

_____

_____

_____

_____

_____

_____

_____

_____

MY RATING
How did you like the movie?

☆ ☆ ☆ ☆ ☆

Title:

Date: _____

Where I watched it:

_____

Who I watched with:

_____

_____

My Favorite Character:

_____

My Favorite Scene:

_____

_____

_____

My Favorite Line:

> "
>
>   "

My Favorite Song:

_____

MOVIE GENRE

What kind of movie was it?

- [ ] Animation/Cartoon
- [ ] Comedy
- [ ] Science Fiction
- [ ] Action/Adventure
- [ ] Fantasy/Superhero
- [ ] Horror/Suspense Thriller
- [ ] Drama
- [ ] Musical
- [ ] Romantic Comedy
- [ ] Documentary

My thoughts:

_____

_____

_____

_____

_____

_____

_____

_____

MY RATING

How did you like the movie?

☆ ☆ ☆ ☆ ☆

Title:

Date: _____

Where I watched it:
_____

Who I watched with:
_____
_____

My Favorite Character:
_____

My Favorite Scene:
_____
_____
_____

My Favorite Line:

"

"

My Favorite Song:
_____

MOVIE GENRE
What kind of movie was it?

- ☐ Animation/Cartoon
- ☐ Comedy
- ☐ Science Fiction
- ☐ Action/Adventure
- ☐ Fantasy/Superhero
- ☐ Horror/Suspense Thriller
- ☐ Drama
- ☐ Musical
- ☐ Romantic Comedy
- ☐ Documentary

popcorn

My thoughts:
_____
_____
_____
_____
_____
_____
_____
_____
_____

MY RATING
How did you like the movie?

☆ ☆ ☆ ☆ ☆

Title:

Date:

Where I watched it:
_____

Who I watched with:
_____
_____

My Favorite Character:
_____

My Favorite Scene:
_____
_____
_____
_____

My Favorite Line:

"

"

My Favorite Song:
_____

MOVIE GENRE

What kind of movie was it?

- ☐ Animation/Cartoon
- ☐ Comedy
- ☐ Science Fiction
- ☐ Action/Adventure
- ☐ Fantasy/Superhero
- ☐ Horror/Suspense Thriller
- ☐ Drama
- ☐ Musical
- ☐ Romantic Comedy
- ☐ Documentary

popcorn

My thoughts:
_____
_____
_____
_____
_____
_____
_____
_____
_____

MY RATING

How did you like the movie?

☆ ☆ ☆ ☆ ☆

Title:

Date: _____

Where I watched it:
_____

Who I watched with:
_____
_____

My Favorite Character:
_____

My Favorite Scene:
_____
_____
_____

My Favorite Line:

"

                              "

My Favorite Song:
_____

What kind of movie was it?

- ☐ Animation/Cartoon
- ☐ Comedy
- ☐ Science Fiction
- ☐ Action/Adventure
- ☐ Fantasy/Superhero
- ☐ Horror/Suspense Thriller
- ☐ Drama
- ☐ Musical
- ☐ Romantic Comedy
- ☐ Documentary

My thoughts:
_____
_____
_____
_____
_____
_____
_____
_____
_____

MY RATING
How did you like the movie?

☆ ☆ ☆ ☆ ☆

Title:

Date:

Where I watched it:
_____

Who I watched with:
_____
_____

My Favorite Character:
_____

My Favorite Scene:
_____
_____
_____
_____

My Favorite Line:

"

"

My Favorite Song:
_____

MOVIE GENRE
What kind of movie was it?
- [ ] Animation/Cartoon
- [ ] Comedy
- [ ] Science Fiction
- [ ] Action/Adventure
- [ ] Fantasy/Superhero
- [ ] Horror/Suspense Thriller
- [ ] Drama
- [ ] Musical
- [ ] Romantic Comedy
- [ ] Documentary

popcorn

My thoughts:
_____
_____
_____
_____
_____
_____
_____

MY RATING
How did you like the movie?

☆ ☆ ☆ ☆ ☆

Title:

Date: _____

Where I watched it:

_____

Who I watched with:

_____

_____

My Favorite Character:

_____

My Favorite Scene:

_____

_____

_____

_____

My Favorite Line:

"

                              ">

My Favorite Song:

_____

MOVIE GENRE
What kind of ___ was it?

- ☐ Animation/___on
- ☐ Comedy
- ☐ Science Fictio___
- ☐ Action/Advent___
- ☐ Fantasy/Superhe___
- ☐ Horror/Suspense ___er
- ☐ Drama
- ☐ Musical
- ☐ Romantic Comedy
- ☐ Documentary

My thoughts:

_____

_____

_____

_____

_____

_____

_____

_____

_____

MY RATING
How did you like the movie?

☆ ☆ ☆ ☆ ☆

Title:

Date: _____

Where I watched it: _____
_____

Who I watched with: _____
_____

My Favorite Character: _____
_____

My Favorite Scene: _____
_____
_____
_____
_____
_____

My Favorite Line:

"

"

My Favorite Song: _____
_____

MOVIE GENRE

What kind of movie was it?

- ☐ Animation/Cartoon
- ☐ Comedy
- ☐ Science Fiction
- ☐ Action/Adventure
- ☐ Fantasy/Superhero
- ☐ Horror/Suspense Thriller
- ☐ Drama
- ☐ Musical
- ☐ Romantic Comedy
- ☐ Documentary

popcorn

My thoughts:
_____
_____
_____
_____
_____
_____
_____
_____
_____

MY RATING

How did you like the movie?

☆ ☆ ☆ ☆ ☆

Title:

Date: _____

Where I watched it:

_____

Who I watched with:

_____

_____

My Favorite Character:

_____

My Favorite Scene:

_____

_____

_____

_____

My Favorite Line:

"

                                    "

My Favorite Song:

_____

MOVIE GENRE

What kind of movie was it?

☐ Animation/Cartoon
☐ Comedy
☐ Science Fiction
☐ Action/Adventure
☐ Fantasy/Superhero
☐ Horror/Suspense Thriller
☐ Drama
☐ Musical
☐ Romantic Comedy
☐ Documentary

My thoughts:

_____

_____

_____

_____

_____

_____

_____

_____

_____

_____

MY RATING

How did you like the movie?

☆ ☆ ☆ ☆ ☆

Title:

Date:

Where I watched it:

Who I watched with:

My Favorite Character:

My Favorite Scene:

My Favorite Line:

"

"

My Favorite Song:

MOVIE GENRE
What kind of movie was it?

- [ ] Animation/Cartoon
- [ ] Comedy
- [ ] Science Fiction
- [ ] Action/Adventure
- [ ] Fantasy/Superhero
- [ ] Horror/Suspense Thriller
- [ ] Drama
- [ ] Musical
- [ ] Romantic Comedy
- [ ] Documentary

My thoughts:

MY RATING
How did you like the movie?

☆ ☆ ☆ ☆ ☆

Title:

Date: _____

Where I watched it:

_____

Who I watched with:

_____

_____

My Favorite Character:

_____

My Favorite Scene:

_____

_____

_____

My Favorite Line:

"

"

My Favorite Song:

_____

MOVIE GENRE

What kind of movie was it?

- ☐ Animation/Cartoon
- ☐ Comedy
- ☐ Science Fiction
- ☐ Action/Adventure
- ☐ Fantasy/Superhero
- ☐ Horror/Suspense Thriller
- ☐ Drama
- ☐ Musical
- ☐ Romantic Comedy
- ☐ Documentary

My thoughts:

_____
_____
_____
_____
_____
_____
_____
_____
_____
_____

MY RATING

How did you like the movie?

☆ ☆ ☆ ☆ ☆

Title:

Date:

Where I watched it:

Who I watched with:

My Favorite Character:

My Favorite Scene:

My Favorite Line:

"

"

My Favorite Song:

MOVIE GENRE
What kind of movie was it?

- [ ] Animation/Cartoon
- [ ] Comedy
- [ ] Science Fiction
- [ ] Action/Adventure
- [ ] Fantasy/Superhero
- [ ] Horror/Suspense Thriller
- [ ] Drama
- [ ] Musical
- [ ] Romantic Comedy
- [ ] Documentary

popcorn

My thoughts:

MY RATING
How did you like the movie?

☆ ☆ ☆ ☆ ☆

Title:

Date: _____

Where I watched it:

_____

Who I watched with:

_____

_____

My Favorite Character:

_____

My Favorite Scene:

_____

_____

_____

My Favorite Line:

> "
>
> "

My Favorite Song:

_____

My thoughts:

_____

_____

_____

_____

_____

_____

_____

_____

_____

MY RATING

How did you like the movie?

☆ ☆ ☆ ☆ ☆

Title:

Date:

Where I watched it:

Who I watched with:

My Favorite Character:

My Favorite Scene:

My Favorite Line:

"
"

My Favorite Song:

MOVIE GENRE

What kind of movie was it?

- ☐ Animation/Cartoon
- ☐ Comedy
- ☐ Science Fiction
- ☐ Action/Adventure
- ☐ Fantasy/Superhero
- ☐ Horror/Suspense Thriller
- ☐ Drama
- ☐ Musical
- ☐ Romantic Comedy
- ☐ Documentary

My thoughts:

popcorn

MY RATING

How did you like the movie?

☆ ☆ ☆ ☆ ☆

Title:

Date: _____

Where I watched it:

_____

Who I watched with:

_____

_____

My Favorite Character:

_____

My Favorite Scene:

_____

_____

_____

_____

My Favorite Line:

"
              "

My Favorite Song:

_____

MOVIE GENRE
What kind of movie was it?

☐ Animation/Cartoon
☐ Comedy
☐ Science Fiction
☐ Action/Adventure
☐ Fantasy/Superhero
☐ Horror/Suspense Thriller
☐ Drama
☐ Musical
☐ Romantic Comedy
☐ Documentary

My thoughts:

_____
_____
_____
_____
_____
_____
_____
_____
_____
_____
_____

MY RATING
How did you like the movie?

☆ ☆ ☆ ☆ ☆

Title:

Date: _____

Where I watched it:

_____

Who I watched with:

_____

_____

My Favorite Character:

_____

My Favorite Scene:

_____

_____

_____

_____

My Favorite Line:

"

"

My Favorite Song:

_____

MOVIE GENRE
What kind of movie was it?

- [ ] Animation/Cartoon
- [ ] Comedy
- [ ] Science Fiction
- [ ] Action/Adventure
- [ ] Fantasy/Superhero
- [ ] Horror/Suspense Thriller
- [ ] Drama
- [ ] Musical
- [ ] Romantic Comedy
- [ ] Documentary

popcorn

My thoughts:

_____

_____

_____

_____

_____

_____

_____

_____

MY RATING
How did you like the movie?

☆ ☆ ☆ ☆ ☆

Title:

Date: _____

Where I watched it:

_____

Who I watched with:

_____

_____

My Favorite Character:

_____

My Favorite Scene:

_____

_____

_____

_____

My Favorite Line:

"

               "

My Favorite Song:

_____

MOVIE GENRE
What kind of movie was it?

- [ ] Animation/Cartoon
- [ ] Comedy
- [ ] Science Fiction
- [ ] Action/Adventure
- [ ] Fantasy/Superhero
- [ ] Horror/Suspense Thriller
- [ ] Drama
- [ ] Musical
- [ ] Romantic Comedy
- [ ] Documentary

My thoughts:

_____

_____

_____

_____

_____

_____

_____

_____

MY RATING
How did you like the movie?

☆ ☆ ☆ ☆ ☆

Title:

Date:

Where I watched it:

_____

Who I watched with:

_____

_____

My Favorite Character:

_____

My Favorite Scene:

_____

_____

_____

_____

My Favorite Line:

"

                                »

My Favorite Song:

_____

MOVIE GENRE
What kind of movie was it?

- [ ] Animation/Cartoon
- [ ] Comedy
- [ ] Science Fiction
- [ ] Action/Adventure
- [ ] Fantasy/Superhero
- [ ] Horror/Suspense Thriller
- [ ] Drama
- [ ] Musical
- [ ] Romantic Comedy
- [ ] Documentary

popcorn

My thoughts:

_____

_____

_____

_____

_____

_____

_____

_____

MY RATING
How did you like the movie?

☆ ☆ ☆ ☆ ☆

Title: _____

Date: _____

Where I watched it: _____
_____

Who I watched with: _____
_____
_____

My Favorite Character: _____
_____

My Favorite Scene: _____
_____
_____
_____
_____

My Favorite Line:

"

"

My Favorite Song: _____
_____

MOVIE GENRE
What kind of movie was it?

- [ ] Animation/Cartoon
- [ ] Comedy
- [ ] Science Fiction
- [ ] Action/Adventure
- [ ] Fantasy/Superhero
- [ ] Horror/Suspense Thriller
- [ ] Drama
- [ ] Musical
- [ ] Romantic Comedy
- [ ] Documentary

popcorn

My thoughts: _____
_____
_____
_____
_____
_____
_____
_____
_____

MY RATING
How did you like the movie?

☆ ☆ ☆ ☆ ☆

Title:

Date:

Where I watched it:

_____

Who I watched with:

_____

_____

My Favorite Character:

_____

My Favorite Scene:

_____

_____

_____

_____

My Favorite Line:

"

                    "

My Favorite Song:

_____

MOVIE GENRE
What kind of movie was it?

- [ ] Animation/Cartoon
- [ ] Comedy
- [ ] Science Fiction
- [ ] Action/Adventure
- [ ] Fantasy/Superhero
- [ ] Horror/Suspense Thriller
- [ ] Drama
- [ ] Musical
- [ ] Romantic Comedy
- [ ] Documentary

popcorn

My thoughts:

_____

_____

_____

_____

_____

_____

_____

_____

_____

_____

MY RATING
How did you like the movie?

☆ ☆ ☆ ☆ ☆

Title:

Date: _____

Where I watched it:

_____

Who I watched with:

_____

_____

My Favorite Character:

_____

My Favorite Scene:

_____

_____

_____

My Favorite Line:

"

                              "

My Favorite Song:

_____

MOVIE GENRE

What kind of movie was it?

- ☐ Animation/Cartoon
- ☐ Comedy
- ☐ Science Fiction
- ☐ Action/Adventure
- ☐ Fantasy/Superhero
- ☐ Horror/Suspense Thriller
- ☐ Drama
- ☐ Musical
- ☐ Romantic Comedy
- ☐ Documentary

My thoughts:

_____

_____

_____

_____

_____

_____

_____

_____

_____

MY RATING

How did you like the movie?

☆ ☆ ☆ ☆ ☆

Title:

Date:

Where I watched it:

_____

Who I watched with:

_____

_____

My Favorite Character:

_____

My Favorite Scene:

_____

_____

_____

_____

My Favorite Line:

"

                                »

My Favorite Song:

_____

MOVIE GENRE
What kind of movie was it?

- [ ] Animation/Cartoon
- [ ] Comedy
- [ ] Science Fiction
- [ ] Action/Adventure
- [ ] Fantasy/Superhero
- [ ] Horror/Suspense Thriller
- [ ] Drama
- [ ] Musical
- [ ] Romantic Comedy
- [ ] Documentary

My thoughts:

_____

_____

_____

_____

_____

_____

_____

_____

_____

_____

MY RATING
How did you like the movie?

☆ ☆ ☆ ☆ ☆

Title:

Date: _____

Where I watched it:

_____

Who I watched with:

_____

_____

My Favorite Character:

_____

My Favorite Scene:

_____

_____

_____

_____

My Favorite Line:

"

"

My Favorite Song:

_____

MOVIE GENRE
What kind of movie was it?

- ☐ Animation/Cartoon
- ☐ Comedy
- ☐ Science Fiction
- ☐ Action/Adventure
- ☐ Fantasy/Superhero
- ☐ Horror/Suspense Thriller
- ☐ Drama
- ☐ Musical
- ☐ Romantic Comedy
- ☐ Documentary

My thoughts:

_____

_____

_____

_____

_____

_____

_____

_____

_____

MY RATING
How did you like the movie?

☆ ☆ ☆ ☆ ☆

Title:

Date:

Where I watched it:

_____

Who I watched with:

_____

_____

My Favorite Character:

_____

My Favorite Scene:

_____

_____

_____

_____

My Favorite Line:

> "
>
>   "

My Favorite Song:

_____

MOVIE GENRE
What kind of movie was it?

- ☐ Animation/Cartoon
- ☐ Comedy
- ☐ Science Fiction
- ☐ Action/Adventure
- ☐ Fantasy/Superhero
- ☐ Horror/Suspense Thriller
- ☐ Drama
- ☐ Musical
- ☐ Romantic Comedy
- ☐ Documentary

popcorn

My thoughts:

_____

_____

_____

_____

_____

_____

_____

_____

_____

_____

MY RATING
How did you like the movie?

☆ ☆ ☆ ☆ ☆

Title:

Date: _____

Where I watched it:
_____

Who I watched with:
_____
_____

My Favorite Character:
_____

My Favorite Scene:
_____
_____
_____
_____

My Favorite Line:
"
                          "

My Favorite Song:
_____

MOVIE GENRE
What kind of movie was it?

- [ ] Animation/Cartoon
- [ ] Comedy
- [ ] Science Fiction
- [ ] Action/Adventure
- [ ] Fantasy/Superhero
- [ ] Horror/Suspense Thriller
- [ ] Drama
- [ ] Musical
- [ ] Romantic Comedy
- [ ] Documentary

My thoughts:
_____
_____
_____
_____
_____
_____
_____
_____
_____

MY RATING
How did you like the movie?

☆ ☆ ☆ ☆ ☆

Title:

Date:

Where I watched it:

_____

Who I watched with:

_____

_____

My Favorite Character:

_____

My Favorite Scene:

_____

_____

_____

_____

My Favorite Line:

"

"

My Favorite Song:

_____

MOVIE GENRE
What kind of movie was it?

- [ ] Animation/Cartoon
- [ ] Comedy
- [ ] Science Fiction
- [ ] Action/Adventure
- [ ] Fantasy/Superhero
- [ ] Horror/Suspense Thriller
- [ ] Drama
- [ ] Musical
- [ ] Romantic Comedy
- [ ] Documentary

popcorn

My thoughts:

_____

_____

_____

_____

_____

_____

_____

_____

_____

MY RATING
How did you like the movie?

☆ ☆ ☆ ☆ ☆

Title:

Date: _____

Where I watched it:

_____

Who I watched with:

_____

_____

My Favorite Character:

_____

My Favorite Scene:

_____

_____

_____

My Favorite Line:

"

"

My Favorite Song:

_____

MOVIE GENRE
What kind of movie was it?

- ☐ Animation/Cartoon
- ☐ Comedy
- ☐ Science Fiction
- ☐ Action/Adventure
- ☐ Fantasy/Superhero
- ☐ Horror/Suspense Thriller
- ☐ Drama
- ☐ Musical
- ☐ Romantic Comedy
- ☐ Documentary

My thoughts:

_____

_____

_____

_____

_____

_____

_____

MY RATING
How did you like the movie?

☆ ☆ ☆ ☆ ☆

Title:

Date:

Where I watched it:

_____

Who I watched with:

_____

_____

My Favorite Character:

_____

My Favorite Scene:

_____

_____

_____

_____

My Favorite Line:

"

»

My Favorite Song:

_____

MOVIE GENRE
What kind of movie was it?

☐ Animation/Cartoon
☐ Comedy
☐ Science Fiction
☐ Action/Adventure
☐ Fantasy/Superhero
☐ Horror/Suspense Thriller
☐ Drama
☐ Musical
☐ Romantic Comedy
☐ Documentary

popcorn

My thoughts:

_____

_____

_____

_____

_____

_____

_____

_____

_____

MY RATING
How did you like the movie?

☆ ☆ ☆ ☆ ☆

Title:

Date: _____

Where I watched it:

_____

Who I watched with:

_____

_____

My Favorite Character:

_____

My Favorite Scene:

_____

_____

_____

_____

My Favorite Line:

" _____ "

My Favorite Song:

_____

MOVIE GENRE
What kind of movie was it?

- ☐ Animation/Cartoon
- ☐ Comedy
- ☐ Science Fiction
- ☐ Action/Adventure
- ☐ Fantasy/Superhero
- ☐ Horror/Suspense Thriller
- ☐ Drama
- ☐ Musical
- ☐ Romantic Comedy
- ☐ Documentary

popcorn

My thoughts:

_____

_____

_____

_____

_____

_____

_____

_____

_____

MY RATING
How did you like the movie?

☆ ☆ ☆ ☆ ☆

Title:

Date:

Where I watched it:

_____

Who I watched with:

_____

_____

My Favorite Character:

_____

My Favorite Scene:

_____

_____

_____

_____

My Favorite Line:

"

          »

My Favorite Song:

_____

MOVIE GENRE
What kind of movie was it?

- [ ] Animation/Cartoon
- [ ] Comedy
- [ ] Science Fiction
- [ ] Action/Adventure
- [ ] Fantasy/Superhero
- [ ] Horror/Suspense Thriller
- [ ] Drama
- [ ] Musical
- [ ] Romantic Comedy
- [ ] Documentary

popcorn

My thoughts:

_____

_____

_____

_____

_____

_____

_____

_____

_____

_____

MY RATING
How did you like the movie?

☆ ☆ ☆ ☆ ☆

Title:

Date: _____

Where I watched it:

_____

Who I watched with:

_____

_____

My Favorite Character:

_____

My Favorite Scene:

_____

_____

_____

My Favorite Line:

"

"

My Favorite Song:

_____

MOVIE GENRE

What kind of movie was it?

- ☐ Animation/Cartoon
- ☐ Comedy
- ☐ Science Fiction
- ☐ Action/Adventure
- ☐ Fantasy/Superhero
- ☐ Horror/Suspense Thriller
- ☐ Drama
- ☐ Musical
- ☐ Romantic Comedy
- ☐ Documentary

popcorn

My thoughts:

_____

_____

_____

_____

_____

_____

_____

_____

MY RATING

How did you like the movie?

☆ ☆ ☆ ☆ ☆

Title:

Date:

Where I watched it:
_____

Who I watched with:
_____
_____

My Favorite Character:
_____

My Favorite Scene:
_____
_____
_____

My Favorite Line:
> "

>>

My Favorite Song:
_____

MOVIE GENRE
What kind of movie was it?

- [ ] Animation/Cartoon
- [ ] Comedy
- [ ] Science Fiction
- [ ] Action/Adventure
- [ ] Fantasy/Superhero
- [ ] Horror/Suspense Thriller
- [ ] Drama
- [ ] Musical
- [ ] Romantic Comedy
- [ ] Documentary

My thoughts:
_____
_____
_____
_____
_____
_____
_____
_____
_____
_____

MY RATING
How did you like the movie?

☆ ☆ ☆ ☆ ☆

Title:

Date: _____

Where I watched it: _____

_____

Who I watched with: _____

_____

_____

My Favorite Character: _____

_____

My Favorite Scene: _____

_____

_____

_____

_____

My Favorite Line:

"

"

My Favorite Song: _____

_____

MOVIE GENRE
What kind of movie was it?

- [ ] Animation/Cartoon
- [ ] Comedy
- [ ] Science Fiction
- [ ] Action/Adventure
- [ ] Fantasy/Superhero
- [ ] Horror/Suspense Thriller
- [ ] Drama
- [ ] Musical
- [ ] Romantic Comedy
- [ ] Documentary

My thoughts: _____

_____

_____

_____

_____

_____

_____

_____

_____

_____

_____

MY RATING
How did you like the movie?

☆ ☆ ☆ ☆ ☆

Title:

Date:

Where I watched it:
_____

Who I watched with:
_____
_____

My Favorite Character:
_____

My Favorite Scene:
_____
_____
_____
_____

My Favorite Line:

    "

                            "

My Favorite Song:
_____

MOVIE GENRE
What kind of movie was it?

- [ ] Animation/Cartoon
- [ ] Comedy
- [ ] Science Fiction
- [ ] Action/Adventure
- [ ] Fantasy/Superhero
- [ ] Horror/Suspense Thriller
- [ ] Drama
- [ ] Musical
- [ ] Romantic Comedy
- [ ] Documentary

popcorn

My thoughts:
_____
_____
_____
_____
_____
_____
_____
_____
_____

MY RATING
How did you like the movie?

☆ ☆ ☆ ☆ ☆

Title:

Date: _____

Where I watched it:

_____

Who I watched with:

_____

_____

My Favorite Character:

_____

My Favorite Scene:

_____

_____

_____

_____

My Favorite Line:

"

„„

My Favorite Song:

_____

MOVIE GENRE
What kind of movie was it?

- ☐ Animation/Cartoon
- ☐ Comedy
- ☐ Science Fiction
- ☐ Action/Adventure
- ☐ Fantasy/Superhero
- ☐ Horror/Suspense Thriller
- ☐ Drama
- ☐ Musical
- ☐ Romantic Comedy
- ☐ Documentary

My thoughts:

_____

_____

_____

_____

_____

_____

_____

_____

_____

MY RATING
How did you like the movie?

☆ ☆ ☆ ☆ ☆

Title:

Date: _____

Where I watched it:
_____

Who I watched with:
_____
_____

My Favorite Character:
_____

My Favorite Scene:
_____
_____
_____
_____

My Favorite Line:

"

                    "

My Favorite Song:
_____

MOVIE GENRE
What kind of movie was it?

- [ ] Animation/Cartoon
- [ ] Comedy
- [ ] Science Fiction
- [ ] Action/Adventure
- [ ] Fantasy/Superhero
- [ ] Horror/Suspense Thriller
- [ ] Drama
- [ ] Musical
- [ ] Romantic Comedy
- [ ] Documentary

popcorn

My thoughts:
_____
_____
_____
_____
_____
_____
_____
_____
_____

MY RATING
How did you like the movie?

☆ ☆ ☆ ☆ ☆

Title:

Date: _____

Where I watched it:
_____

Who I watched with:
_____
_____

My Favorite Character:
_____

My Favorite Scene:
_____
_____
_____
_____

My Favorite Line:

"
"

My Favorite Song:
_____

MOVIE GENRE
What kind of movie was it?

- [ ] Animation/Cartoon
- [ ] Comedy
- [ ] Science Fiction
- [ ] Action/Adventure
- [ ] Fantasy/Superhero
- [ ] Horror/Suspense Thriller
- [ ] Drama
- [ ] Musical
- [ ] Romantic Comedy
- [ ] Documentary

My thoughts:
_____
_____
_____
_____
_____
_____
_____

MY RATING
How did you like the movie?

☆ ☆ ☆ ☆ ☆

MOVIE REVIEW JOURNAL FOR KIDS

Title:

Date:

Where I watched it:

Who I watched with:

My Favorite Character:

My Favorite Scene:

My Favorite Line:

" "

My Favorite Song:

MOVIE GENRE
What kind of movie was it?

- [ ] Animation/Cartoon
- [ ] Comedy
- [ ] Science Fiction
- [ ] Action/Adventure
- [ ] Fantasy/Superhero
- [ ] Horror/Suspense Thriller
- [ ] Drama
- [ ] Musical
- [ ] Romantic Comedy
- [ ] Documentary

popcorn

My thoughts:

MY RATING
How did you like the movie?

☆ ☆ ☆ ☆ ☆

Title:

Date: _____

Where I watched it:

_____

Who I watched with:

_____

_____

My Favorite Character:

_____

My Favorite Scene:

_____

_____

_____

My Favorite Line:

"

                              "

My Favorite Song:

_____

MOVIE GENRE
What kind of movie was it?

- ☐ Animation/Cartoon
- ☐ Comedy
- ☐ Science Fiction
- ☐ Action/Adventure
- ☐ Fantasy/Superhero
- ☐ Horror/Suspense Thriller
- ☐ Drama
- ☐ Musical
- ☐ Romantic Comedy
- ☐ Documentary

My thoughts:

_____

_____

_____

_____

_____

_____

_____

_____

MY RATING
How did you like the movie?

☆ ☆ ☆ ☆ ☆

Title:

Date:

Where I watched it:

Who I watched with:

My Favorite Character:

My Favorite Scene:

My Favorite Line:

"

"

My Favorite Song:

MOVIE GENRE
What kind of movie was it?

- [ ] Animation/Cartoon
- [ ] Comedy
- [ ] Science Fiction
- [ ] Action/Adventure
- [ ] Fantasy/Superhero
- [ ] Horror/Suspense Thriller
- [ ] Drama
- [ ] Musical
- [ ] Romantic Comedy
- [ ] Documentary

My thoughts:

popcorn

MY RATING
How did you like the movie?

☆ ☆ ☆ ☆ ☆

Title:

Date: _____

What kind of movie was it?

Where I watched it:

☐ Animation/Cartoon
☐ Comedy
☐ Science Fiction
☐ Action/Adventure

Who I watched with:

☐ Fantasy/Superhero
☐ Horror/Suspense Thriller
☐ Drama
☐ Musical
☐ Romantic Comedy
☐ Documentary

My Favorite Character:

My thoughts:

My Favorite Scene:

popcorn

My Favorite Line:

"

"

My Favorite Song:

MY RATING

How did you like the movie?

☆ ☆ ☆ ☆ ☆

Title:

Date:

Where I watched it:

_____

Who I watched with:

_____

_____

My Favorite Character:

_____

My Favorite Scene:

_____

_____

_____

My Favorite Line:

> "
>
>   "

My Favorite Song:

_____

MOVIE GENRE
What kind of movie was it?

- [ ] Animation/Cartoon
- [ ] Comedy
- [ ] Science Fiction
- [ ] Action/Adventure
- [ ] Fantasy/Superhero
- [ ] Horror/Suspense Thriller
- [ ] Drama
- [ ] Musical
- [ ] Romantic Comedy
- [ ] Documentary

My thoughts:

_____

_____

_____

_____

_____

_____

_____

_____

_____

MY RATING
How did you like the movie?

☆ ☆ ☆ ☆ ☆

Title:

Date: _____

Where I watched it:

_____

Who I watched with:

_____

_____

My Favorite Character:

_____

My Favorite Scene:

_____

_____

_____

My Favorite Line:

"

                            ”

My Favorite Song:

_____

MOVIE GENRE
What kind of movie was it?

- ☐ Animation/Cartoon
- ☐ Comedy
- ☐ Science Fiction
- ☐ Action/Adventure
- ☐ Fantasy/Superhero
- ☐ Horror/Suspense Thriller
- ☐ Drama
- ☐ Musical
- ☐ Romantic Comedy
- ☐ Documentary

My thoughts:

_____

_____

_____

_____

_____

_____

_____

_____

MY RATING
How did you like the movie?

☆ ☆ ☆ ☆ ☆

Title:

Date:

Where I watched it:

_____

Who I watched with:

_____

_____

My Favorite Character:

_____

My Favorite Scene:

_____

_____

_____

_____

My Favorite Line:

"

"

My Favorite Song:

_____

MOVIE GENRE
What kind of movie was it?

- [ ] Animation/Cartoon
- [ ] Comedy
- [ ] Science Fiction
- [ ] Action/Adventure
- [ ] Fantasy/Superhero
- [ ] Horror/Suspense Thriller
- [ ] Drama
- [ ] Musical
- [ ] Romantic Comedy
- [ ] Documentary

My thoughts:

_____

_____

_____

_____

_____

_____

_____

_____

_____

_____

MY RATING
How did you like the movie?

☆ ☆ ☆ ☆ ☆

Title:

Date: _____

Where I watched it:
_____

Who I watched with:
_____
_____

My Favorite Character:
_____

My Favorite Scene:
_____
_____
_____

My Favorite Line:

"

"

My Favorite Song:
_____

MOVIE GENRE
What kind of movie was it?

- ☐ Animation/Cartoon
- ☐ Comedy
- ☐ Science Fiction
- ☐ Action/Adventure
- ☐ Fantasy/Superhero
- ☐ Horror/Suspense Thriller
- ☐ Drama
- ☐ Musical
- ☐ Romantic Comedy
- ☐ Documentary

My thoughts:
_____
_____
_____
_____
_____
_____
_____
_____

MY RATING
How did you like the movie?

☆ ☆ ☆ ☆ ☆

Title:

Date:

Where I watched it:

_____

Who I watched with:

_____

_____

My Favorite Character:

_____

My Favorite Scene:

_____

_____

_____

_____

My Favorite Line:

"

                    "

My Favorite Song:

_____

MOVIE GENRE
What kind of movie was it?

☐ Animation/Cartoon
☐ Comedy
☐ Science Fiction
☐ Action/Adventure
☐ Fantasy/Superhero
☐ Horror/Suspense Thriller
☐ Drama
☐ Musical
☐ Romantic Comedy
☐ Documentary

My thoughts:

_____

_____

_____

_____

_____

_____

_____

_____

_____

MY RATING
How did you like the movie?

☆ ☆ ☆ ☆ ☆

Title:

Date: _____

Where I watched it:
_____

Who I watched with:
_____
_____

My Favorite Character:
_____

My Favorite Scene:
_____
_____
_____
_____

My Favorite Line:

"

"

My Favorite Song:
_____

MOVIE GENRE
What kind of movie was it?

- [ ] Animation/Cartoon
- [ ] Comedy
- [ ] Science Fiction
- [ ] Action/Adventure
- [ ] Fantasy/Superhero
- [ ] Horror/Suspense Thriller
- [ ] Drama
- [ ] Musical
- [ ] Romantic Comedy
- [ ] Documentary

popcorn

My thoughts:
_____
_____
_____
_____
_____
_____
_____
_____
_____
_____

MY RATING
How did you like the movie?

☆ ☆ ☆ ☆ ☆

Title:

Date:

Where I watched it:

_____

Who I watched with:

_____

_____

My Favorite Character:

_____

My Favorite Scene:

_____

_____

_____

_____

My Favorite Line:

"

"

My Favorite Song:

_____

MOVIE GENRE
What kind of movie was it?

- [ ] Animation/Cartoon
- [ ] Comedy
- [ ] Science Fiction
- [ ] Action/Adventure
- [ ] Fantasy/Superhero
- [ ] Horror/Suspense Thriller
- [ ] Drama
- [ ] Musical
- [ ] Romantic Comedy
- [ ] Documentary

My thoughts:

_____

_____

_____

_____

_____

_____

_____

_____

_____

MY RATING
How did you like the movie?

☆ ☆ ☆ ☆ ☆

popcorn

Title:

Date: _____

Where I watched it:

_____

Who I watched with:

_____

_____

My Favorite Character:

_____

My Favorite Scene:

_____

_____

_____

My Favorite Line:

" _____

_____

_____

» _____

My Favorite Song:

_____

MOVIE GENRE

What kind of movie was it?

- ☐ Animation/Cartoon
- ☐ Comedy
- ☐ Science Fiction
- ☐ Action/Adventure
- ☐ Fantasy/Superhero
- ☐ Horror/Suspense Thriller
- ☐ Drama
- ☐ Musical
- ☐ Romantic Comedy
- ☐ Documentary

My thoughts:

_____

_____

_____

_____

_____

_____

_____

_____

_____

MY RATING

How did you like the movie?

☆ ☆ ☆ ☆ ☆

Title:

Date:

Where I watched it:

_____

Who I watched with:

_____

_____

My Favorite Character:

_____

My Favorite Scene:

_____

_____

_____

_____

My Favorite Line:

"

                            "

My Favorite Song:

_____

MOVIE GENRE
What kind of movie was it?

- [ ] Animation/Cartoon
- [ ] Comedy
- [ ] Science Fiction
- [ ] Action/Adventure
- [ ] Fantasy/Superhero
- [ ] Horror/Suspense Thriller
- [ ] Drama
- [ ] Musical
- [ ] Romantic Comedy
- [ ] Documentary

popcorn

My thoughts:

_____

_____

_____

_____

_____

_____

_____

_____

_____

_____

MY RATING
How did you like the movie?

☆ ☆ ☆ ☆ ☆

Title: _____

Date: _____

Where I watched it:
_____
_____

Who I watched with:
_____
_____

My Favorite Character:
_____

My Favorite Scene:
_____
_____
_____
_____

My Favorite Line:

" _____

_____ "

My Favorite Song:
_____

MOVIE GENRE
What kind of movie was it?
- [ ] Animation/Cartoon
- [ ] Comedy
- [ ] Science Fiction
- [ ] Action/Adventure
- [ ] Fantasy/Superhero
- [ ] Horror/Suspense Thriller
- [ ] Drama
- [ ] Musical
- [ ] Romantic Comedy
- [ ] Documentary

My thoughts:
_____
_____
_____
_____
_____
_____
_____
_____
_____

MY RATING
How did you like the movie?
☆ ☆ ☆ ☆ ☆

Title:

Date:

Where I watched it:

_____

Who I watched with:

_____

_____

My Favorite Character:

_____

My Favorite Scene:

_____

_____

_____

_____

My Favorite Line:

"

"

My Favorite Song:

_____

MOVIE GENRE
What kind of movie was it?

- [ ] Animation/Cartoon
- [ ] Comedy
- [ ] Science Fiction
- [ ] Action/Adventure
- [ ] Fantasy/Superhero
- [ ] Horror/Suspense Thriller
- [ ] Drama
- [ ] Musical
- [ ] Romantic Comedy
- [ ] Documentary

popcorn

My thoughts:

_____

_____

_____

_____

_____

_____

_____

_____

_____

MY RATING
How did you like the movie?

☆ ☆ ☆ ☆ ☆

Title: _____

Date: _____

Where I watched it:
_____

Who I watched with:
_____
_____

My Favorite Character:
_____

My Favorite Scene:
_____
_____
_____

My Favorite Line:

"
                              "

My Favorite Song:
_____

MOVIE GENRE
What kind of movie was it?

- [ ] Animation/Cartoon
- [ ] Comedy
- [ ] Science Fiction
- [ ] Action/Adventure
- [ ] Fantasy/Superhero
- [ ] Horror/Suspense Thriller
- [ ] Drama
- [ ] Musical
- [ ] Romantic Comedy
- [ ] Documentary

popcorn

My thoughts:
_____
_____
_____
_____
_____
_____
_____
_____
_____

MY RATING
How did you like the movie?

☆ ☆ ☆ ☆ ☆

Title:

Date:

Where I watched it:

_____

Who I watched with:

_____

_____

My Favorite Character:

_____

My Favorite Scene:

_____

_____

_____

_____

My Favorite Line:

"

"

My Favorite Song:

_____

- [ ] Animation/Cartoon
- [ ] Comedy
- [ ] Science Fiction
- [ ] Action/Adventure
- [ ] Fantasy/Superhero
- [ ] Horror/Suspense Thriller
- [ ] Drama
- [ ] Musical
- [ ] Romantic Comedy
- [ ] Documentary

popcorn

My thoughts:

_____

_____

_____

_____

_____

_____

_____

_____

_____

MY RATING
How did you like the movie?

☆ ☆ ☆ ☆ ☆

Made in the USA
Middletown, DE
19 October 2022

13105786R00066